Musings On The Lounge

Edward Bertrand Finck

In the interest of creating a more extensive selection of rare historical book reprints, we have chosen to reproduce this title even though it may possibly have occasional imperfections such as missing and blurred pages, missing text, poor pictures, markings, dark backgrounds and other reproduction issues beyond our control. Because this work is culturally important, we have made it available as a part of our commitment to protecting, preserving and promoting the world's literature. Thank you for your understanding.

Musings on the Lounge

By Bert Finck

JOHN P. MORTON & COMPANY
INCORPORATED
LOUISVILLE, KENTUCKY

Copyright, 1914
by BERT FINCK

Musings on the Lounge

Most all of us need guides, not judges; nurses, not jails; infirmaries, not prisons; not punishment, but cures. Many a sin has been committed through exhaustion; and many through the fever of despair; many through the wild hunger-pangs for love and sympathy—it takes maddest presumption to condemn.

All in this world must battle, you may know: some, with the sword; some, with the shield; some, with their patience; some, with their wit; some, with the cap and bells of the fool; some, with the medicine-bottle; some, with the crutch.

We see and we hear nature with the eyes and ears of our heart's mood; even as we are, so nature is; morning to me is night, perhaps, to you; my night may be your morn. Unto the broken-hearted, spring is a sad

Musings on the Lounge

part of the year, for it tells of sprouting hopes that very soon will fade away; unto the conscience-stricken, rain-drops are the tears of remorse; while to bright buoyant innocence, there is music in the rustling of dry leaves. The despondent hears a sigh in the bird's rejoicing, and he beholds a shadow in each beam; the waters speak, but they are always moaning; the winds tell of ethereal tragedies. The stars, which to some are brilliant signals of hope, to others are the bright, cruel emblems of fate, indifferent to the life or death of worlds and ages; while the moon, inspirer of romance and love, can heartlessly smile upon miseries. "Be true! be true!" is the continuous song of nature; but to him that has been faithless, it chants a dirge for a lost soul.

I always did love flowers; that is, wild and the common garden flowers; those which awaken with the spring, and fall asleep with the autumn. Hot-house flowers bear the odor of artificiality like so many people that I know; pretty, perhaps, but not healthily so, bearing a kind of feverish attraction.

Musings on the Lounge

Curious are these people, even interesting —fascinating, for a short while; but, too often, that which is called originality, is perversity; not rarely, glossy degeneration itself. Wit may be the sharp tooth of innate bitterness; entertaining conversation; the network of fraud; animation may be assisted by an opiate; and interest in every one may be interest in none. Give me the man or woman who is natural—who is truly original, and he or she will not create much attention in the world. It is the feverish, the unhealthy, that attract for a glittering moment, and then pass, soon forgotten, out of the way. The true, the real, move along unnoticed, but when they are gone there is a vacancy in the circle where they moved. Give me the wild and common garden flowers that fall asleep with the autumn, and awaken with the spring; give me the hearts that are natural and true, for they fall asleep when their work is done, and awaken again.

My money's gone. What does it matter? We are here to-day and dead to-morrow. It matters not how foolishly I spent it; it

Musings on the Lounge

is not in my possession, and it does somebody good. But this is what concerns me—what most terribly concerns me—the words that I have uttered and that can not be recalled. They are not in my possession, and they do somebody harm. The money that I lost is gone from me forever; and what difference, when I die, whether I own one coin or two? But the words that I have uttered are but lost from my possession; they are mine, without the power to control or call them back. The money that I lost may bring pleasure to another, but brings it joy or sorrow, it will perish with this life. But the words that I have uttered meet me in eternity.

The night is dark, without a single star; so is my life, without a ray of hope. But in the blackness comes a roving wind, whispering mysterious sympathy; so in my life's deep gloom a wandering spirit tells of unseen guidance through my misery.

It is easy to philosophize when your heart is bright with ideals; but who can moralize or muse with shattered dreams? Who can

Musings on the Lounge

contemplate in the midst of ghosts, or theorize in the tombs of murdered hopes? What man can speculate upon eternity, when on this earth his love has been betrayed, and he cares not if he ever lives again, for that which would make a new world sweet can not be there? What soul would yearn for an unending life, were there no soul it longed to meet again? What is the worth of this life, or another, if it gives no gold of precious sentiment?

You'll often find that men assail the vice which they in secret are most guilty of; while sometimes they that laugh at kindly deeds, in hidden corners, weep from sympathy.

What we call industry is sometimes a feverish flight of souls from the presence of ghosts: souls flee from accusing visions that pursue, into the strong arms of labor, and attain a virtue by means of their fears.

Many a glorious deed that illumines the pages of history; many a work of art that

Musings on the Lounge

inspires the heart-throbs of life; many an eloquent word that rescues from hell and despair—was conceived by yearning spirits or remorse.

In every club, in each organization, there is a hidden traitor who will one day show his fangs. A Judas sits at each assembly-table, ready with kiss to barter or betray.

Many a word of wisdom has been uttered by folly's remorse; many a picture of Heaven has been painted by yearning spirits of hell.

Beware of him that calls himself reformer; his soul is often filled with gilded cunning to crush those evils that bring him no profit, and spread the ones he thinks will nourish him.

Some write for glory; some, for coin; some, for enjoyment; some, for relief; some, from belief that they have a message; some, just because they are fools; some, because they can not help but write, whether they will or no.

Musings on the Lounge

Many a crime has been committed for the sake of a noble purpose. Many a man has robbed in order to pay a debt, or to avoid a loved one's distress. Desperate honor or generosity may go mad.

There are those who would be glad to die, did they think that they could read their obituaries; and to die in the most violent manner, were they sure that they could hear the cry of "Extra."

There is charity that is done for atonement; there is charity that is done for spite; there is charity that is done through vain glory; there is charity that is done from tact; but the charity that is loved by the angels, is that which comes without a motive, from the heart.

How cold it is to-night! how cold it is! cold as adversity! The winds howl like hungry creditors, who would devour the very bones of a shivering debtor, and drive him off the earth. Cold as the charity of success that casts contempt

Musings on the Lounge

on failure; or as the mercy of a passionless breast toward them that have erred through warmth of passion. The trees stand gaunt and bare, like poverty surrounded by pitiless need. How cold it is to-night! Cold as soulless policy, that chills all warmth of sentiment, affection, flowery youth, leaving but bleak ambition where gentleness has been. How cold it is to-night! Cold as the indifference of the world to individual sorrow; cold—cold as pessimism, that sees good in no man; cold as the blast of dire necessity upon ethereal aims; cold as the icy breath of guilt that freezes the pleasures of life, cold—cold as knowledge when devoid of gentle pity, or as philosophy unmixed with kindly dreams; cold—cold as unloved fame, or wealth when it is friendless; cold—cold as selfishness, that makes the world a winter's night.

I hear in the distance the voice of the sea, and I think I hear a child that is crying for a mother—for an angel that it saw once in a dream. But it is only the voice of the sea. I hear a maiden calling for her lost love to

Musings on the Lounge

return—parted from her by proud passion and mistake. But it is only the voice of the sea. Another poet's heart is surely breaking from neglect! I can hear it—I can hear it—break, break, break! But it is only the voice of the sea. I hear an old man moaning o'er the ruins of his youth, o'er bright prospects turned to ghostly carnival. But it is only the voice of the sea. I hear a sob for mercy from wild spirits of remorse, and the answer, furious answer of despair. But it is only the voice of the sea. I hear a grave lamenting that it was deceived by death—that death gave it but a shadow, not a life. But it is only the voice of the sea. I hear a laugh of triumph o'er the tragic rhapsody, and I hear music from the rustling wings of hope. But it is only the voice of the sea.

When we realize how much sin is committed through ill-health; how much through heredity and unhappy circumstances of life; how much through natural craving of starved hearts for affection; how much through the sickness of despair—we can

Musings on the Lounge

readily perceive how easy it was for Christ to forgive sinners; Christ, the pinnacle of all philosophy.

There are times when the sunshine is mockery; there would be more sympathy in the roarings of the winds; the hills tell of naught but unsatisfied yearnings; the sky tells of naught but eternal unrest.

Let us remember this, as we turn aside from the wrong-doer: A happy person never yet has done a wrong, and let us rather pity than condemn.

It takes courage to bear the abuse of the world; it takes greater courage to bear the praise of the world; but it takes the greatest courage of all to bear the world's neglect.

What we call indolence may be sometimes hopelessness; eccentricity, efforts of pride to conceal; affectation, self-conscious ignorance; frivolity, care gone mad.

Many fall into vice through weakness; many, through curiosity; many, through

Musings on the Lounge

wild searchings for refuge; many, through unsatisfied longings for sympathy and cheer; many, through the feverish cravings of disease; and many through exhaustion, sinking to rest upon soft spots along the way—spots that are infested with flowery poison.

Oh come to me, birds of the air! Tell me of hopes of other lands! Tell me of those who have gone from me, and yet who tenderly think of me! Tell me of words that you have heard from angels floating through the skies with souls that they have borne away from the tragedies of earth! Tell me of words that you have heard from sweet celestial sympathy falling upon the ears of those traveling to Paradise! Tell me of comfort and of cheer given by God's winged messengers unto the burdens in their arms saved from life's wintry ills! Tell me of comfort for the sinner in prospect of redemption—grace, and opportunity for atonement in the great intermediate state! Tell me of cheer for the remorseful! Tell me of cheer for injured hearts! For the dead are wise and therefore generous—wronger and wronged become reconciled. Tell me of hope for us abandoned, by those we love, on this plane below! Tell me how the faithful departed ceaselessly wait and pray for us! Tell me in simple words the truth sages have yearned for all these years—that Eternity is filled with love and charity and hope!

There's a voice in the distance calling me; there's a hand in the distance beckoning me; there's a smile in the distance lighting my way. Oh, angel of Death, I come to thee! The voice is the same that has often called me; the hand is the same that oft beckoned to me; the smile is the same that has often thrilled me. Oh, angel of Death, I come to thee! The voice I have heard in the chants of the air; I have followed the hand in the evening shades; the smile I have seen in the rays of the dawn. Oh, angel of Death, I come to thee!

The devils only fight for souls that are worth fighting for; the greatest sinners could have been the greatest saints.

Musings on the Lounge

Many sin through worry; many, through pain; many, through delirium; many, through despair.

Sometimes a dream-drop falls upon our parched hearts, and brings to life a dying flower there.

The world is ghastly with the shades of tragedies; but the most uncanny shade of all is that of suicided self-respect.

Not all the honors showered on your head; not all the ribbons pinned upon your breast; not all the world's goods heaped about your feet—can shut out ghosts of murdered self-respect.

Death is the liberator of our imprisoned better selves; death is the restorer of all things real.

No fire can warm the chilliness of guilt; no breeze can cool the fever of remorse.

Christ, the height of wisdom, is also height of charity.

Musings on the Lounge

The path to wisdom often leads through folly; the road to Heaven sometimes leads through hell.

Feel not resentful or aggrieved at acts of the ungrateful, but rather pity them as those of minds mad or diseased. Weep for ingratitude as you would weep for wretched idiocy, or want of light; and give it not your loathing but your tears.

Affectation is sometimes our refuge; a mask to hide our defects.

There are those who pay their debts through fear; there are those who pay their debts through pride; not all are honest from nobility of soul.

Mistakes that we have made in life arise before us like diabolical spectres; and what we call remorse may be their freezing the warmth of our conceit, and showing to us our folly.

A man can be honest, and yet be cruel; a man can be diligent, and yet be unjust; a

Musings on the Lounge

man can be pious, and yet be intolerant; but he can not be charitable and have very dark faults; for the halo of his charity is reflected on them all.

Of all the tragedies that come to us in life, there's none so great as loss of self-respect.

The noblest deeds are sometimes those that were caused by the remorse of bad ones.

Death is the end of misunderstanding; death is the beginning of explanation.

Many sins and vices come from sickness and disease; God will look on them as the ragings of fever.

What we call sullenness may be defiant embarrassment.

We fear the people we have wronged, and through our fears we learn to hate them.

What is work but the materialization of dreams? According to the dreams, is the work.

Musings on the Lounge

There are those who might overlook an insult to themselves, but who, if even a dog they loved were hit, would seek their cudgels.

Why is man so prone to worry? Because it is an idle thing to do; and there is nothing in this world so fascinating as idleness to the human mind.

There are in some of us such dark, unholy spirits, that we ourselves do fear to look at them; and as we see them boldly in another, we dread that person as we would a looking-glass, which shows the ugly features we would hide.

Do we ever stop to think of the dead who are still on earth? Of the unburied, stalking dead? There is a precious comfort in caring for the graves of the blessed departed, and in praying for the repose of their souls; but where is the comfort in beholding the cold unburied dead, and in hearing the rattling of their bones? For they before whose tomb we kneel belonged to us, and still belong to us, and they are forever a part of our world; but they who move about us, dead, were once ours, but now are gone, and there are no flowers that we can strew on their mounds, and no prayers that we can say for their rest. We built our dreams about them; our fortunes were wrecked for them; we gave up true gold for the sake of their glitter, and discovered, too late, our mistake; and instead of ideals, love, and friendship, in our faces skeletons grin. Oh, to be envied are they who can kneel at the shrines of the sacred departed, knowing that their love is unchanged. But they are to be pitied, indeed, whose dead walk in their midst, without shrines and without prayers for their repose!

Many flee to vice as a refuge from madness, and commit sins to save themselves from committing crimes.

In this life there is not so much wickedness as madness; not so much vice as disease; not so much faithlessness as weakness. The world is in need of wise physicians and good nurses—of guidance and sympathy—

Musings on the Lounge

for the sick, the wounded and demented, who, in their frenzy and anguish, commit wild acts, for which they receive blows, instead of treatment.

When we are able to pity the robber as well as the robbed, the murderer the same as the murdered; when we can feel that the ingrate needs our sympathy's balm as much as does the heart which he has wounded—only then are we beginning to ascend the steep path which leads up to the height of wisdom.

Creditors are chasing him, to tear the tatters that he wears from off his body. (Fiercer far than wolves are creditors!) What can he do but run, until he falls exhausted to the ground? They snatch his rags, and then they walk disappointedly away. What have they gained by chasing him? What has he gained by running away? Far better had they all sat down and watched the passers-by.

There are natures that arouse the evil within us as soon as they enter our presence.

Musings on the Lounge

Unselfish prayers ascend to God like welcome incense, but selfish prayers are blasphemous and despised.

Is a wolf at your door? Invite him in, and he'll soon turn and stalk away.

The trouble is, that we never pull out a weed from our nature, but that we pull out with it a flower too. How often does reformation mean destruction!

There are moments in the lives of each of us—wild, fearful moments—when we feel, no matter how good we may have been, no matter how bad we may have been, that we have been living in the shadows of mistake; wild, fearful moments, these, on the waves of which ride demons, mocking the folly of our past, and casting weird regret in the breasts of saints as well as sinners.

There are those that are thoughtlessly selfish, and there are those that are thoughtfully selfish. There may be attractions in the thoughtlessly selfish, but the thoughtfully selfish are repulsive.

Musings on the Lounge

Dreamers can never be lonely, for angels or devils are with them all the time.

What is called sin is often the hysteria of suffering.

There's the recklessness of optimism, and the recklessness of despair.

Death speaks the words that life in vain would say.

Life is mystical; life is weird; life is filled with miracles. Ghosts and goblins prowl about; angels glide in their midst to defeat them.

The rogue admonishing the rogue, the thief condemning the thief, the madman confining the madman, make some of the queer sights of life.

Bright minds have been dulled by education, and souls have been murdered by homilies.

Heaven is reached only through struggles with hell.

Musings on the Lounge

There are sometimes disguised angels in the realms of hell, ready even there, unperceived, to save us.

To reach heights, we must first have touched depths.

Who can so realize the glory of virtue as he that has struggled out of the mire of depravity?

Souls have been saved from sin by sinners; the devil's own agents oft betray him.

The bigot, no matter how good he may be, can bring more grief to this world than the villain.

This is the tragic part of every reformation —the good is oft uprooted with the bad.

The grandest paintings that the world has ever seen; the grandest poems that the world has ever read; the grandest music that the world has ever heard, were created by the spirits of remorse.

Musings on the Lounge

No matter how good we may be, no matter how bad we may be, there are times when our hearts are shadowed by mysterious regret.

When you can weep for the sins and the errors of the world—only then have you reached true height.

There are flowers among the weeds of every disposition—wild flowers, it is true, but more beautiful oft than cultivated ones. It is hard, sometimes, to say which should be called weeds and which termed flowers— what shall be praised as a virtue, and what condemned as a vice.

Not all that wear crosses are Christians; not all that wear Masonic charms are Masons; not all that carry swords are warriors; not all that bear sceptres are kings.

THE ACTRESS.

All day long, you see her smiling—all day long. (All day long, her heart is breaking— all day long.)

Musings on the Lounge

All day long you hear her chirping like a bird without a care. (All day long, her soul is moaning o'er the ashes of dead dreams.)

THE TWO MOURNERS.

The one came, in rich, heavy mourning, and lay a gorgeous bunch of roses on a grave, and said "I am glad this is over; I must hasten now to try on my new gown!" The other came, without mourning or veil, and dropped a single flower on the grave, and said, as she wiped away a tear from her eye, "I can never forget his kindness to me."

THE FLOWER.

Only a flower, crushed on the way, trampled on, spat upon, by the hurrying crowd. Once it was blooming fair as the dawn; it gave a moment's pleasure, and was cast to the ground. So is the mortal that lives for this world; short is his glory, tossed aside, and despised. Oh, look not for gratitude or for reward for hours of pleasure given to fellowman! Shun the fate of the flower; bloom not for the world.

GHOSTS.

Ghosts of the past arise before me, and scatter dust of buried dreams; ghosts of the present glide between them, and together they begin to dance. What can I do but dance with them, and join their ghostly revelry? But soon as I begin to dance, they turn and fade away from me.

IN PRISON.

There's a beautiful view from my prison window (still, I'm in prison) of valleys and hills and flowery roadways (still, I'm in prison). My cell is brilliantly illuminated (still, I'm in prison) with pictures, books, and statuary (still, I'm in prison). My couch is decked with gems and ribbons (still, I'm in prison) and I envy the beggar below in his tatters (for I'm in prison), stretching forth his hand for a coin to buy shelter (for I'm in prison).

CROWS.

The crows of adversity are flocking about me, and croaking forth worries and cares, in the shape of collectors and sharp disappointments—debts, debts, and no money to pay. I can no more than stare at them, and analyze their looks and criticize their discordant notes, and wonder how long they will last; but even as I study them, they flap their wings and fly away.

SUCCESS.

We must pass by, we must overlook, we must blot out, we must forget. We must not see that which we see; we must not hear that which we hear; we must not feel that which we feel, nor speak that which we know. We must be ever ready to suppress, and to starve to death our hearts.

WORK.

In work we bury all our disappointments, our murdered hopes, and ashes of dead dreams; we flee to work for refuge from wild spectres, and from the shadowy forms of grim remorse. In work we drown the voices of sad yearnings, and dull the throbs of passionate despair; in work we find a veil to hide out memories from accusing visions of our life—mistakes.

A NIGHT.

The night is cold, but not so cold as human selfishness. The night is dark, but not so dark as greed and avarice. There is no wind so merciless, there's no such gloomy shade as the black, wintry, schemes of man to crush his fellowman.

TO A WRONG-DOER.

It matters not what sin you have committed; it matters not what wrong you may have done; I know that pain did follow and proceed it, and I can not condemn, but pity you. No matter for what reason the world scorns you or keeps you caged like a wild beast of prey, I know your plight was caused by some mad spirits born with your soul, and so I weep for you.

NATURE STUDIES.

All that I know of the stars, is that they give to me hope; all that I know of the sea, is that it gives sympathy; all that I know of the flowers, is that they give me sweet tales of God's love; and all that the books would tell me of them, could give me no more than this.

THE DREAMER.

How could he have done otherwise than he did? The dull, blind world, it can not understand! He was a dreamer, and he followed dreams, and stumbled over rocks on earth he did not see.

A PRAYER.

Even as my hopes forsake me, help me, God, to be kind! And as my failures mock me, help me, God, to be kind! And as my powers leave me, help me, God, to be kind! And as cold death stares at me, help me, God, to be kind!

Printed by Libri Plureos GmbH in Hamburg, Germany